The Story of Jon: God is Gracious

The Story of Jon:
God is Gracious

Kathleen Ruth Umland Dale

Paintings by Jonathan Ryan Dale

Dedicated to

Jesus Christ, my Saviour, my Lord. There are not enough words to express my gratitude for all He has done and is doing for Jonathan, my whole family, and I. He is healing Jonathan and teaching us to depend on Him daily. He has taught us about the beauty of the ordinary, the peace that comes when we let Him carry our burdens, and the joy of simply holding His hand.

Thank you Lord Jesus for creating us, never giving up on us, suffering, dying, and rising again for us, and being with us every step of our life's journey. We love you.

Special Thanks to

Dr. Paul Carney, Kelly Sheridan, Debbie Ringdahl, and all of Dr. Carney's staff at Shands Hospital in Gainesville, FL, who have taken excellent care of Jonathan and have been instrumental in Jonny's recovery. Thank you for always believing in and fighting for Jonathan. We love you.

Stanley and Grace Umland, my parents, who encouraged and stood shoulder to shoulder with us through the darkest days. We love and miss you.

Wayne and Betty Dale, Mervin's parents, who encouraged and lifted us up in prayer. We love you.

Mervin, my husband and father of my children, who is my friend, my partner, and my comrade-in-arms as we do daily battle in this world. I love you, and Jonny does, too.

Elizabeth, Justin, Victoria, Devon, Alexandria, Jesse, Teddy, Anthony, Jonathan, Cynthia, Yyzzy, Yao, and Ryan, who are all my children—some by birth, some through marriage to my children, some simply through love and my precious grandchildren: Nicolai, Ivan and Eliana. All of you keep my heart overflowing with joy. You remind me every day that God is good and that He loves me abundantly. I love you more than you can imagine. You are always in my prayers, and you each own a special piece of my heart.

Marlane Soldner, my friend, who visited Jonathan and me at the hospital, brought dinner to my family, prayed for us, and so much more. Thank you for loving my family and me. We love you, too.

All my family and friends, who have loved and prayed for my family through this journey. Thank you. We love you, too.

For we were saved in this hope, but hope that is seen is not hope; for why does one still hope for what he sees? But if we hope for what we do not see, we eagerly wait for *it* with perseverance.

Likewise the Spirit also helps in our weaknesses. For we do not know what we should pray for as we ought, but the Spirit Himself makes intercession for us with groanings which cannot be uttered. Now He who searches the hearts knows what the mind of the Spirit *is,* because He makes intercession for the saints according to *the will of* God.

And we know that all things work together for good to those who love God, to those who are the called according to *His* purpose.

Romans 8:24-28 (NKJV)

This is the story of Jon.
Actually, this is just part of the story of Jon—
as told through his art.

Jon is an artist. He told me so.
He declared,

"I am an artist. It is my job to show people what they cannot see with their eyes."

It is my desire that you see in these pages
joy found by trusting completely in Jesus
and God's strength made perfect in our weakness.

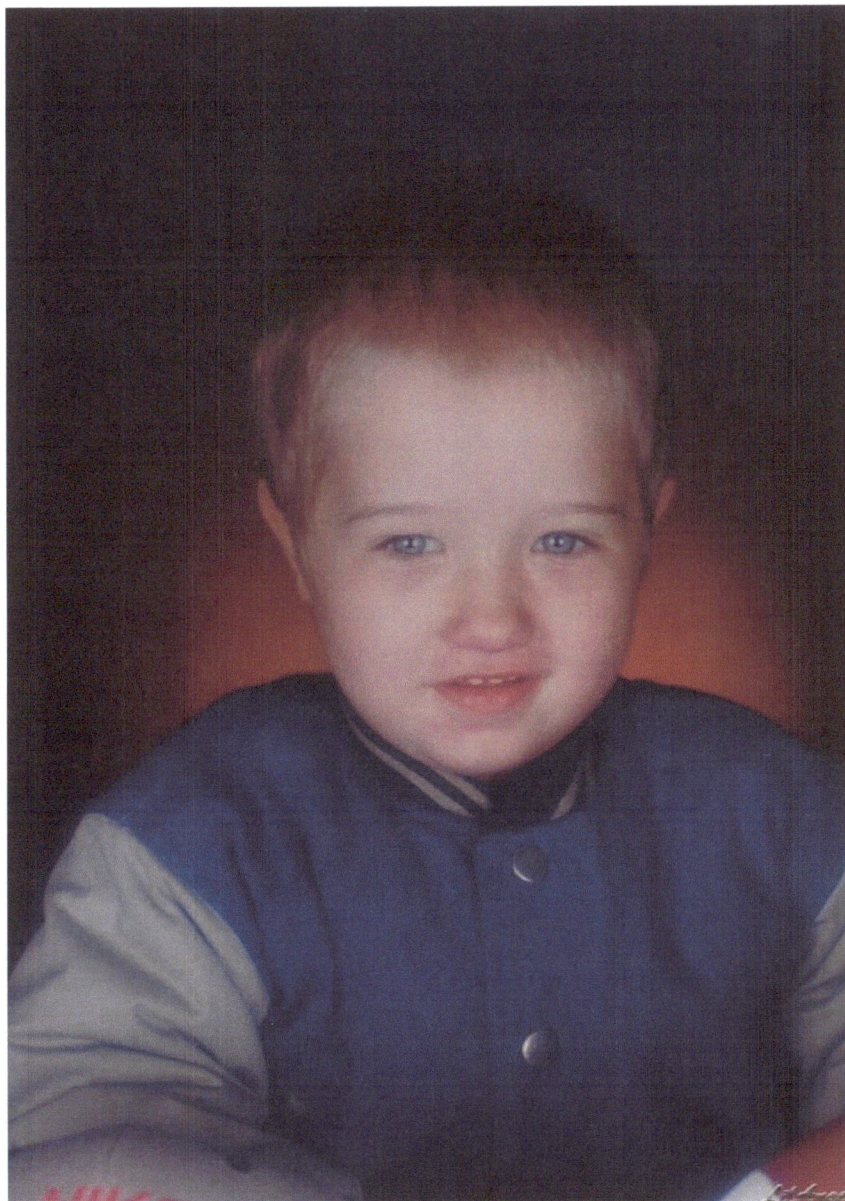

Jonathan Ryan Dale

March 4, 2004: The day before our lives changed forever.

God is Gracious

I sat alone in the hospital room holding our beautiful, precious baby. I looked down at him filled with joy and a little sadness knowing that he would likely be our last. I thought to myself that I would like to keep him little. All my babies were growing up too fast. Elizabeth was already 12 years old; how quickly the time had passed.

A hospital worker came to get the baby's name for his birth certificate. My mind was still foggy from the medication they had given me during the Cesarean section. I couldn't remember what name we had decided on. My mind was completely blank. I called the house, but no one answered because my husband, Merv, was on the way to the hospital. The woman from records insisted that I answer immediately or she would list his name as Male Dale on the birth certificate. I frantically racked my brain trying to remember the name we had decided on, but the only name I could think of was Jonathan Ryan. I was fairly certain that wasn't it. But I told her his name was Jonathan Ryan, and she typed it in.

Merv arrived shortly after she left. I immediately asked him what we were we planning to name the baby. Merv reminded me that we had planned to name him Richard Benjamin after my Uncle Richie and my father.

We asked the woman from hospital records if we could change the name, but she said it was already filed with the state. If we wanted it changed, we would have to file a formal name change with the state. Merv smiled and said to leave it. It was a good name and it suited Jonathan.

Later, I remembered that Jonathan means Jehovah is gracious. Merv and I named our first five children, but God named Jonathan.

Mervin holding Jonathan at the Castillo de San Marcos. March 2000

By age 4, Jonny had a twinkle in his eye, a crooked little grin, and a heart full of mischief. We all knew we were being scammed half the time, but he was irresistible. My eldest son, Teddy, took the training wheels off of Jonny's bike after I told him not to, and Jonny was proudly riding around in circles on the back patio in short order. I couldn't even pretend I was mad when Teddy proudly banged on the glass door to show me. I loved those naughty boys so much.

The next day Jonny had surgery to remove his tonsils and adenoids. The surgery went well, but a hospital mistake left Jonny fighting for his life. For four days we watched his body jump as the ventilator breathed for him. On the fourth day the doctor informed us that he was not doing well; and they were going to remove the ventilator. If Jonny began breathing on his own, he would be fine. If not, they would have to put him back on the ventilator, but he would die. They asked us to leave while they removed the ventilator; we stayed. As soon as they removed the paralytic medication, Jonny began convulsing, and his oxygen levels fell into the thirties. Merv and I just didn't let go of him. The staff helped us move to a couple of chairs then one by one they left the room.

For the next five hours we prayed, read the Bible, and sang praises to honor God; the whole time we held Jonny as he seized. The nurses occasionally came in to check on us. Their fleeting glances and silence spoke volumes. We knew they were waiting for Jonny to die. We didn't know what would happen, but we knew that God was in control. No matter the outcome, God was working everything for good. The greatest miracle we experienced was the incredible peace and joy that filled us as God's presence filled the room. We weren't alone; Jesus was there with us and with Jonny through it all.

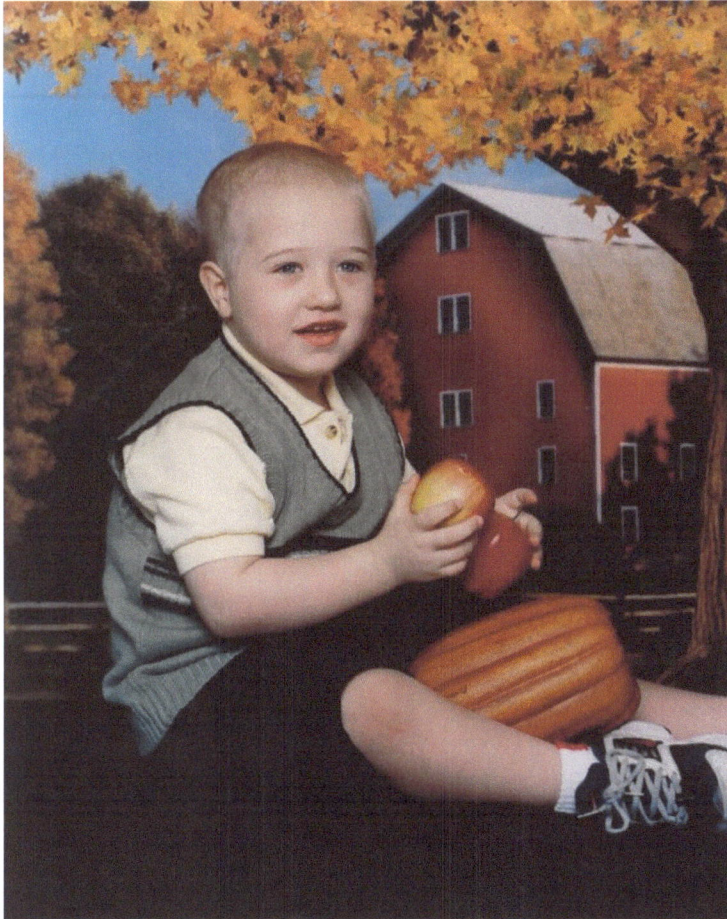

The hospital chaplain stopped by and played a VeggieTales CD. Jonathan suddenly stopped convulsing; he opened his eyes and looked around the room. He closed his eyes again and took a deep breath; his oxygen saturation level immediately began to rise. We watched him as he improved dramatically over the next few hours. The following day, he was moved out of the PICU into a private room.

I thought at any moment my bright-eyed little boy would look up and smile at us, but when he opened his eyes again, they were vacant. My heart broke. He had no muscle control; he couldn't even hold up his head. But Jonny was alive, and that was a miracle. It would not be the last one. God isn't done yet!

If I had been given the choice, I would have chosen an instantaneous healing for Jonathan. God had other plans though, and I trust Him. Jonathan is being healed—just not all at once. God has given us a lifetime worth of miracles for which to praise Him. Jonny can run, play, swim, ride a horse, steer a go-cart and—with great effort—speak. On his thirteenth birthday, Jonny miraculously began to express himself through the gift of painting. Then in 2014, his stories, which either inspired or were inspired by those paintings, began to grow in depth and imagination.

It was nearly Christmas, and I was on the hunt for stocking stuffers when a child's painting set called to me from the shelf. It was no stocking stuffer, and Jonny had too many presents already. As I held it, however, a voice whispered of possibilities. Jonny didn't draw well. He couldn't color within the lines and didn't even know the names of colors, but it just felt right. I bought it against the advice of my other children and decided to save it for Jonny's birthday. Jonny was thrilled with the paint set, and we were amazed by how well he did. We knew it was another miracle.

Jonny painted this fairy princess first.
It may not look impressive, but we collectively held our breath because it was so beautiful.

Painted January 1, 2013

It was more than two weeks before Jonny painted again, and this time the picture came with a story.

Jonny explained that it is a picture of a pirate flag.
He went on to say that the ship's captain was looking up at the flag during the night and using the constellations
to navigate his way to buried treasure!

We were amazed. He was using his imagination to make up his own story, and he had never used words like "constellation" or "navigate" before.

Painted January 18, 2013

Jonny no longer could paint an entire painting in a single day. He was paying more attention to detail, so it took more time. His skill had grown by years in the span of a single month.

This little pampered kitty was so impressive.
The detail was unbelievable.
He carefully chose each color
and lovingly told me about the kitty as she came to life.
Then with a twinkle in his eye he declared,
"I thought I saw a put-ty cat! I did! I did! I did see a put-ty cat!"

Completed February 1, 2013

It was amazing to watch as his brush came right up to the line and then smoothly spread the paint to the next. He was only painting pre-printed pictures, but the fact that he could was breathtaking. A little voice inside my heart whispered again of possibilities.

I smiled. "Are you going to be an artist when you grow up?"

Jonny stopped painting and looked into my eyes coolly. He was defiant. I had insulted him. He replied simply, "I am an artist," and then walked away with an air of dignity.

I could not have felt prouder or loved him more.

Jonny's ice cream sundae picture settled it.
Jonny needed the opportunity to try to paint his own pictures.
No more training wheels!

Completed February 8, 2013

THE
MUSHROOM HOUSE

This is Jon's first real painting.
He drew and painted it all by himself.
It has steps going up and a roller coaster going down
because every house needs a roller coaster!

Completed February 12, 2013

"THE DOCK

goes out into a lake
where you have just tied up your boat.
If you follow the path over the hill and climb the stairs,
you will find Dad waiting there for you."

-Jonny

Completed February 22, 2013

Jonny was excited to have a larger canvas board. He ran from the kitchen table, out the back door, to the apple tree in front of Grandma's house, and then back again. He carefully inspected a certain blossom and counted and recounted its petals on his fingers. I noticed the ladybug wasn't quite even and showed Jonny. He explained, "I know. She is just beginning to open her wings to fly away."

Jonny also told me that the apple blossom he had painted was on the apple tree next to the mushroom house.

Ladybug on an Apple Blossom

This beautiful ladybug is just beginning to open her wings
on the apple tree next to the mushroom house.
She will soon fly away.

Acrylic Painting on 14" x 11" Canvas Board
Completed March 8, 2013

This painting became darker as it took shape. The dark, swirling water and the dark, empty house left you with a feeling of hopelessness and dread. I wondered why he was creating something so foreboding. Then Jonny added the yellow flowers and apples in the trees, and the painting transformed into one of hope.

MY HOUSE

I asked him what it was a picture of,
and his answer made my eyes fill with tears.
"It is my house. Where you and I live,
but nothing is scary if you trust in God."

-Jonny

Jonny used to cry when he could sense a bad seizure was coming. He would try to bury himself in my arms and say, "Monsters are coming!"
Since he painted this picture, he hasn't been afraid any more. He still has seizures, but —praise God!—there are no more monsters. It is my favorite.

Acrylic Painting on 14" x 11" Canvas Board
Completed March 22, 2013

Every picture improved exponentially. I bought Jonny his first real canvas. He spied the texture gels on the paint aisle, and his eye glistened. He touched the samples. "May I please?"

I couldn't resist. I bought him his two favorites. He mixed the glass beads in with the paint then he painted the outer space background of *Dog in Space*. It was brilliant.

Not only were his skills as an artist improving, but the thoughts his paintings expressed were improving as well. His speech and general intellect seemed to be growing by leaps and bounds, but this growth did not come without a price. Jonny's seizures began to worsen.

DOG IN SPACE

This is Jonny's first painting on a real canvas.
After watching *Lost in Space,* Jonny ran over to the table
and got out his brand new canvas and paints.
He declared, "Do-o-og in Spa-a-ace!" before he even began.

Acrylic Painting with Glass Beads on 14" x 11" Canvas
Completed March 28, 2013

CAMPING WITH MY DAD

This is a picture of Jonny camping out under the stars with his dad.
If you look closely, you can see the moon peeking out from behind a tree.
The tent by the water's edge is for Jonny and his dad.
The tent in the background is for his brothers, Teddy and Anthony.
They set up their tents before they went hiking in the mountains.
They are asleep right now, but they will go fishing in the morning.

Acrylic Painting on 14" x 11" Canvas
Completed April 10, 2013

This is the only picture Jonny has painted without drawing it first. He said nothing about the painting, barely looking up from it while he was working on the canvas over the next four days. The fourth day he painted with even more intensity. I became concerned when his hand began to shake and insisted that he take a break. Jonny stood and took one step before falling to the ground with convulsions. It was a bad seizure, and he slept for hours after it had passed. When he woke up, the left side of his face was still drooping, and his left arm and leg were all but useless. However, Jonny was emphatic. He wanted to go to the table and finish his painting immediately. I tried to make him wait until he felt better, but he was determined. Finally, I relented and helped him to the table. He just couldn't rest until he had finished the painting.

GOING HOME

I asked him about the picture, and he looked up at me with tears welling in his eyes, and said, "Going home." Jonny pointed and showed me where home was. It is the yellow linear place at the horizon on the left side of the painting. I knew he was speaking of going home to be with Jesus. Months later, when showing the painting to a visitor, he pointed to the white figures in the sky and explained that it was a picture of him flying home with an angel to Jesus' house.

Acrylic Painting on 20" x 16" Canvas
Completed April 28, 2013

Jonny had us in stitches when he drew what looked like a dinosaur with human legs. When he showed us his drawing, that crooked little grin I love so well spread across his face, and the mischief danced once more in his eyes.

This painting is almost impossible not to touch. He used glass beads to create the dragon's scales and sand to give the castle texture.

Dragon Guarding
Underwater Castle

This is a picture of a peaceful castle resting safely beneath the waves.
What appears to be clouds are actually waves breaking
on the surface of the water.
The inhabitants of the castle have no fear of intruders.
The castle is kept safe by a faithful dragon.
Be careful! It has a poisonous bite.

Mixed Media
Acrylic & Oil Painting with Glass Beads & Sand on 24" x 18" Canvas
Completed September 5, 2013

Jonny began painting without instruction. He had no knowledge of famous artists or the artistic movements they represented.

Jonny's paintings represent how he sees and understands life. They represent his hopes, dreams, and imagination. They tell enchanting tales which his voice still struggles to share.

Unencumbered by the constructs of the correct way to paint, Jonathan has a style that is all his own.

He makes a plan before he begins a painting. Sometimes he begins by drawing a rough picture on a piece of paper. Other times, he draws directly on the canvas. Even his sketches only offer a hint as to what he is creating. It is amazing watching his process which is unique to say the least.

Jonny does not know the names of colors, but he understands them. Jonny places several colors on a single brush. These colors aren't blended. They are each visible on the brush, and when he applies them to the canvas, he uses masterful skill to create such images as the earth in *Dog in Space* and the sky, grass, and river in *Going Home*. There is a brilliance that exists in these impressionistic style paintings that cannot be missed.

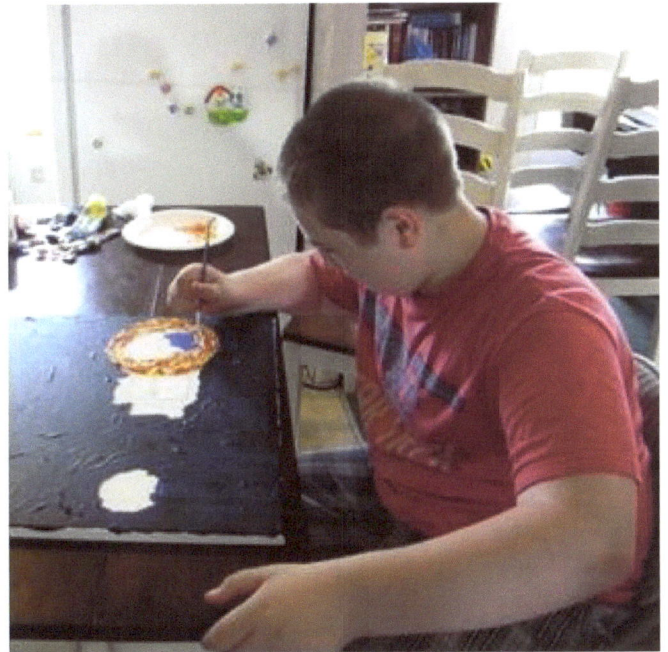

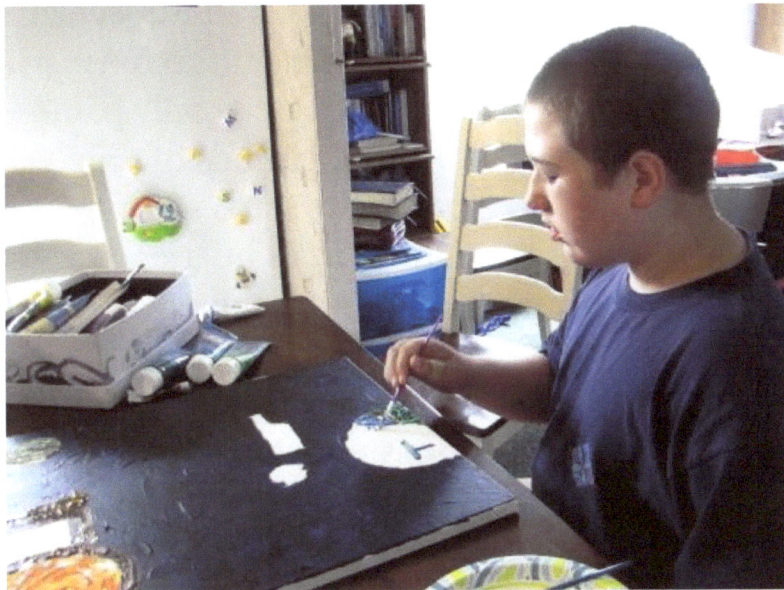

Jonny loves texture. His paintings give you the irresistible desire to touch them. He applies the paint thickly to create depth, so the images actually rise off the canvas, inviting the viewer in.

Jonny prefers acrylic paint because it has a thicker consistency which he can use to sculpt. He typically reserves oil paints for detailed work.

Jonny was very excited to try texture gels he found in the paint aisle. He felt them between his fingers and rubbed them on his skin before trying them out for the first time. Glass beads grace the sky in *Dog in Space* and create the scales of the dragon in *Dragon Guarding Underwater Castle*. Sand was mixed with the paint used on the castle bringing it to life.

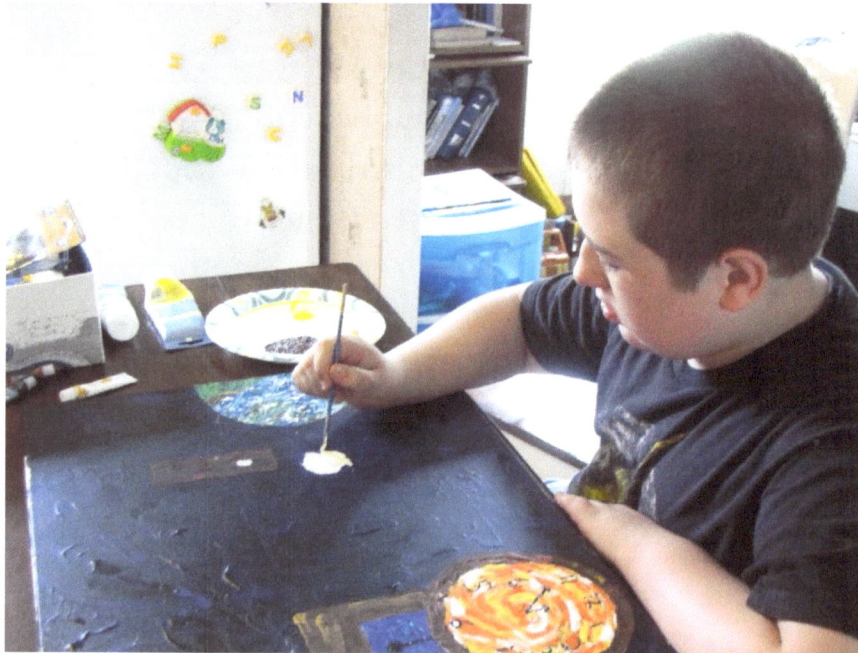

It often takes Jonny weeks or even months to finish a canvas. He can only paint for brief periods of time before he starts seizing. Other times he tries to paint, but his hand shakes so much he has to stop. But Jonny doesn't give up. He is undeterred and keeps at it until he has created exactly the image he desires.

The thoughts Jonathan represents through these paintings are sometimes whimsical and childlike, yet other times he touches on subjects that many adults try to avoid. His paintings express fantasy, fears, humor, and contain an understanding far beyond his years. It is apparent to everyone who meets Jonny that he is full of unconditional love, irrepressible curiosity, unstoppable determination, and a healthy dose of mischief. But it took his paintings and stories to hint at the brilliant mind hidden by his aphasia.

Our pastor preached a sermon about wisdom. He explained how you need to make decisions today not based on where you want to be in ten minutes, but rather on where you want to be in ten years and for all eternity. Jonny must have been paying attention because he came home and began this picture.

He titled it . . .

TIME TO CHOOSE

Mixed Media
Acrylic, Gaucho, & Oil Painting on 24" x 18" Canvas
Completed September 18, 2013

Alien Giraffe riding a Spaceboard

This alien giraffe's spaceship was hit by an asteroid.
He escaped on his spaceboard. Don't worry about him!
Jonny has assured me that he is not far from his home planet.
It is hiding just behind his sun.

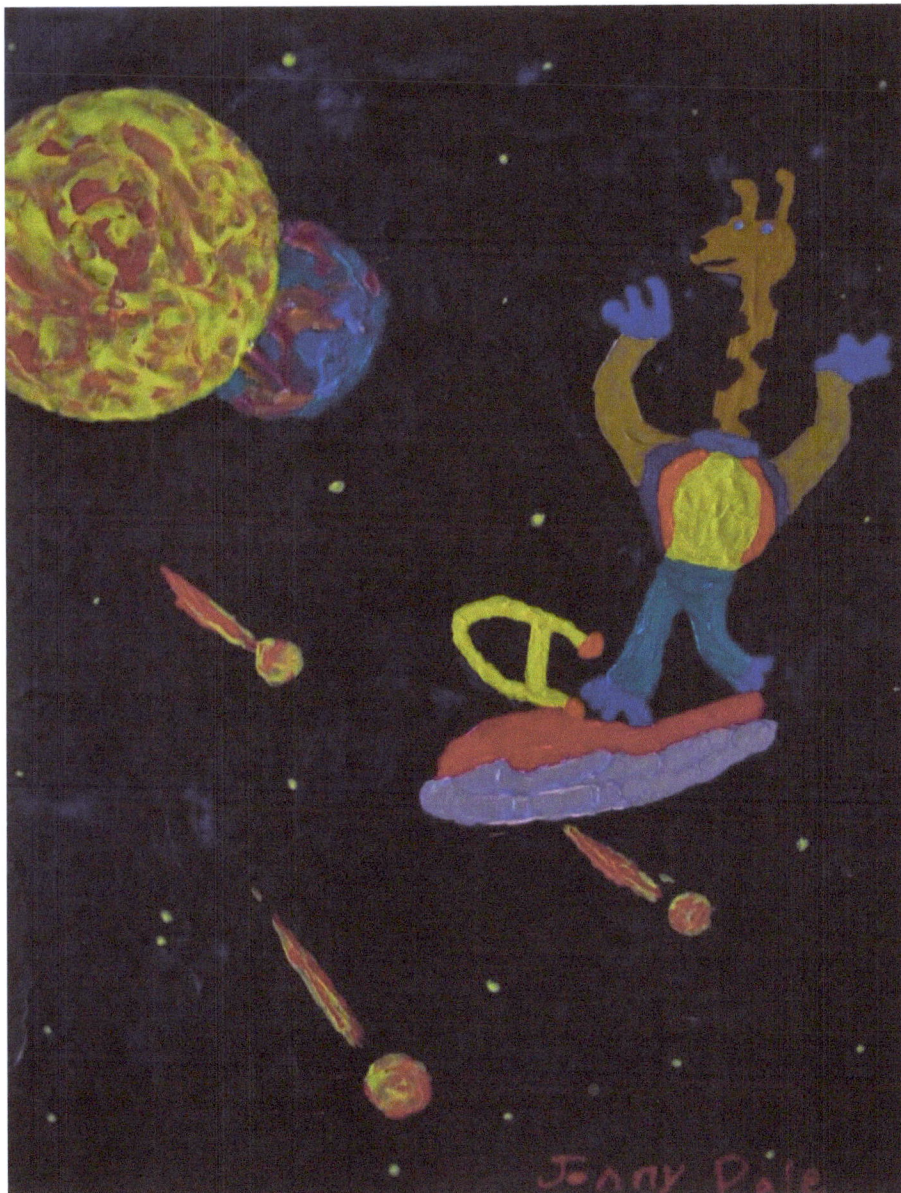

Acrylic Painting on 11" x 14" Canvas
Completed November 6, 2013

Reindeer Pulling Santa's Sons' Sleighs

"Santa lived long ago and . . . no one lives forever. Santa was a good man because he loved Jesus. He liked to give other people presents. These sleighs belong to Santa's sons. His three sons, Jonathan, Teddy, and Anthony gave people presents after he died to honor him and so did their children.

There's not really a naughty and nice list. They just do for everyone they can and especially for children who are in the hospital.

They use lots of sleighs with reindeer who help them make their deliveries. Reindeer are very helpful because they can fly even in bad weather."

-Jonny

Acrylic Painting on 14" x 11" Canvas
Completed February 24, 2014

Jonathan Dale
&
The Battle of the Pirates
of Booha

"This Alien Pirate is from the planet Booha.
He says 'Arrr, Mateys. Attack!!!'
Then he comes running out of the trees towards me."

-Jonny

Acrylic Painting on 7" x 5" Canvas
Completed September 23, 2014

GEORGE
THE
TREASURE FISH

"Don't trust George the treasure fish!
He is a pirate.
He says he will lead you to treasure,
but he won't.
He will lead you to a faraway cave and rob you."

-Jonny

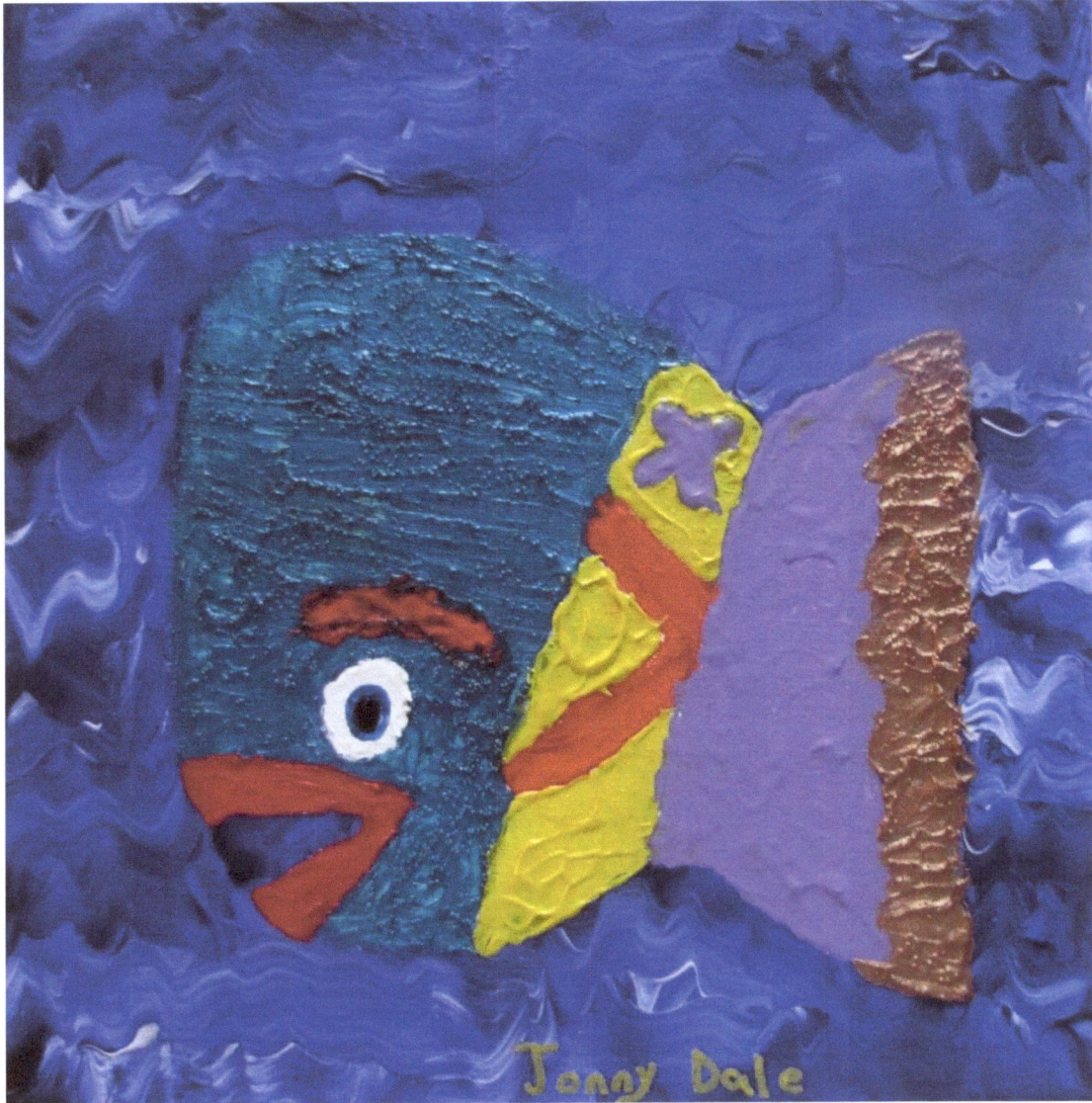

Mixed Media
Acrylic & Oil Painting with Glass Beads on 12" x 12" Canvas
Completed November 21, 2014

Imagine Nation

"Come to Imagine Nation. It is an island in the sky.
You can get there with Mickey or
Take a Viking ship on a river in the air.
If you like you can even set sail with pirates.
Just come.
It is missing you.
I am waiting there for you
And I love you."

-Jonny

Mixed Media
Oil & Acrylic Painting on 12" x 12" Canvas
Completed March 6, 2015

UP! UP and Away!

"Jonny Dale, Mommy, and Daddy
are flying in a balloon into the sky.
We can see over the clouds
and soar higher than the birds.
We are going to take a trip
around the world!
We will see everything!"

-Jonny

Mixed Media
Oil & Acrylic Painting on 20" x 16" Canvas
Completed April 21, 2015

Gene Who

&

the Good Neighbors

"Gene Who, the owl, is going on an adventure. He invented a flyboard.
It can fly fast, faster, and even faster. It has wheels so it can drive on the
ground too. It also has a force-field bubble that covers it
when Gene needs to go under the water—swoosh!

He wants to find a cat named Johann who can sing.
Georgina Squeak, the mouse, is waiting at home for them.
She is baking a cake to celebrate their return.

The friends will travel the world. Gene Who will play the banjo
and Johann and Georgina Squeak will sing.
They will be called "Good Neighbors".

-Jonny

Mixed Media
Acrylic & Oil Painting on 11" x 14" Canvas
Completed November 5, 2015

PETER
HAS A
FLYING PAINTBRUSH

"He is an artist.
He paints trees in the fall and the snow on the pines.
He paints rainbows, sunsets, and clouds in the sky.
He has lots of fun as he flies far from the ground."

-Jonny

Oil Painting on 11" x 14" Canvas
Completed December 3, 2015

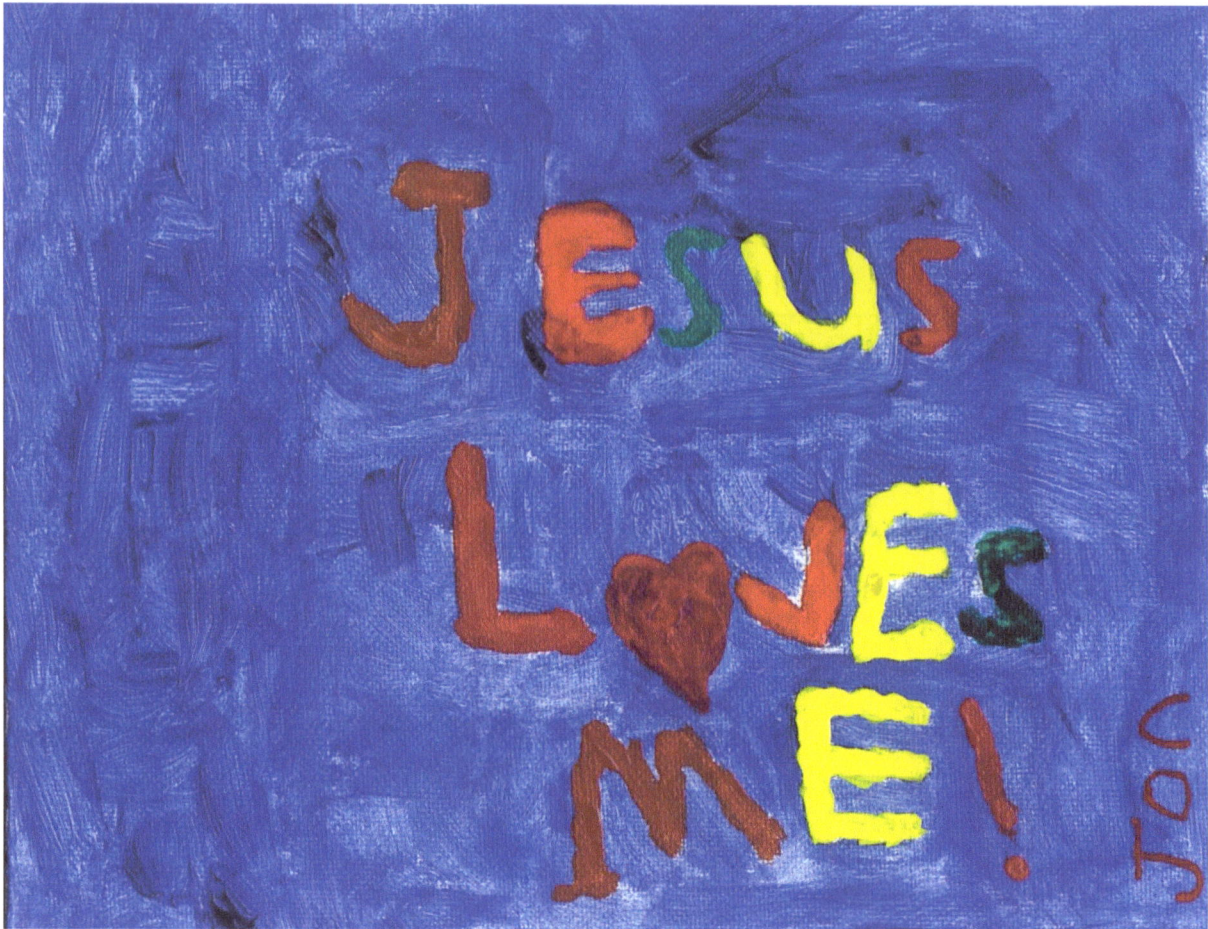

Jonny painted a sign that reads
"Jesus loves me,"
and I know that He does.

Epilogue

2015 has been an exciting year. I can hardly comprehend all that has happened for Jonny.

It began with a segment on our local PBS television station, WJCT. Thank you Stephen Jones, Shannon Greene LeDuke, and Erin O'Connor for giving Jonathan a platform to share his art and story.

Christina SanInocencio, President/Executive Director of the LGS Foundation (Lennox-Gastaut Syndrome), viewed Jonny's PBS segment online and discussed the prospect of working with the LGS Foundation on future events. It also spurred me to start a Kickstarter campaign to publish *The Story of Jon: God is Gracious.* The Kickstarter campaign was successful thanks to our amazing patrons and sponsors who provided us with the material support and encouragement to make this book a reality. Thank you.

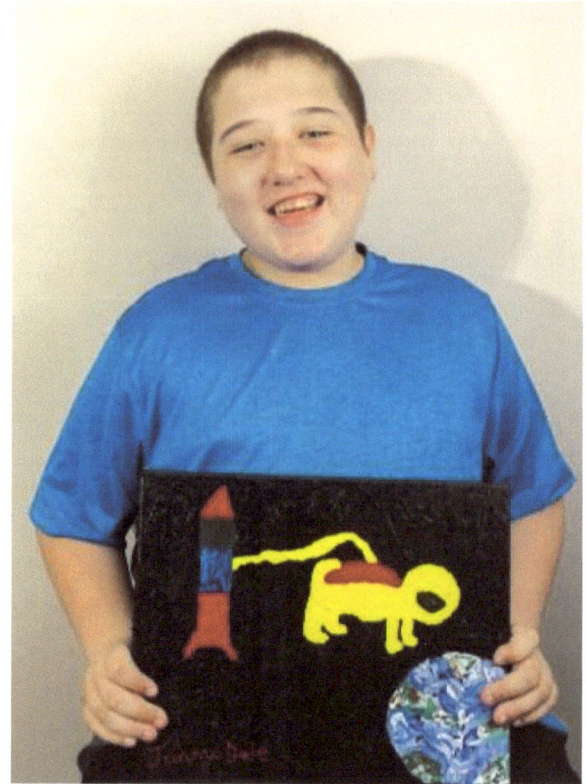

Courtesy of The Lake City Reporter
April 3, 2015

From the beginning, Jonny's recovery has been marked by a series of miracles and setbacks. We have learned to be prepared for anything. Yet we weren't quite ready for the blessing that began on Thursday, April 2, 2015. Jonny was suddenly aphasia-free. Words flowed freely and endlessly from his lips. It began with one well thought-out comment which was followed by another. I was impressed, but Jonny was thrilled. He had to talk about everything he saw and heard. It was beautiful but not earth shattering; the same thing had happen to a lesser degree a couple of weeks earlier. But now I believed the day would come when his aphasia would be a thing of the past. I expected this episode would end as before though—when he fell asleep. He would wake up in the morning once more struggling to express even basic thoughts.

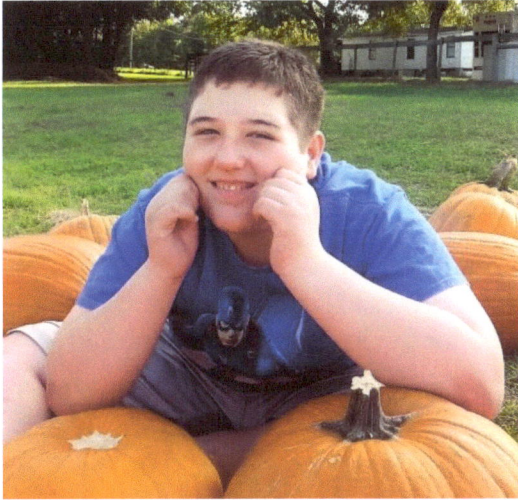

Morning came and Jonathan could still speak; his eyes positively danced. We had interviewed with our local paper, *The Lake City Reporter,* about the art book on Tuesday, and the story was scheduled to run that Sunday. I called them and asked them if I could bring Jonny by. I wanted them to see his transformation. Emily Buchanan, the reporter, said that on a scale from 1 to 10 that Jonny was a 1 Tuesday and a 10 Friday. The editor, Robert Bridges, was amazing and had the article now emphasize all that God had done for Jonny.

By the end of the day, it was apparent that not only was Jonny able to speak, but he was almost a different person. No longer was he disorganized and unable to concentrate on one thing for more than a minute or two. He could hold a real conversation with you. Jonny was polite, funny, and self-assured. That twinkle in his eyes that lit up the room and that crooked grin that he wielded to charm his way into everyone's heart were back. He told me, "I feel so much better!" My heart soared. I had my Jonathan back. In truth, I didn't know he still existed. We had seen glimpses of a brilliant mind when he painted, but the idea that the real Jonathan still existed was beyond my ability to comprehend. He was still little in some ways, but I believed he had the capability to learn.

For the first three days, Jonny could stay quiet for no more than a couple of seconds at a time. Eleven years of near silence needed filling. It was as if a dam had broken, and there was an untamed flood of words rushing forth. But eventually just as flood water settles down and remains within its new boundaries, so Jonny's constant need for conversation settled down. I spent the next week laughing and crying at the same time, all the while praising God.

Friday, April 10, 2015, I knew something was wrong. Jonathan was not quite as well organized. I decided it must be a tonic-clonic seizure brewing. The next day he continued to slip further away. He was disobedient, rude, and pulled on people though he still could speak. We all made excuses for him. Sunday I stayed in the lobby at church with Jonny and watched the service on closed-circuit television. I didn't think he'd be able to sit through a whole service. He made it part way through before he lost interest. Then he had a short tonic-clonic seizure. He was fine, but the last glimpse of my Jonathan slipped back into the fog.

My heart broke. But I was not alone. God was there encouraging me not to give up. If you are running a marathon, you don't quit at the twenty-fifth mile marker no matter how tired you are.

Over the next days, every conversation drifted back to how we had forgotten what life was like before Jonathan's recovery. How quickly we had adjusted to being able to really talk to him. It seemed natural that Jonathan had wanted to and in fact could bathe himself, brush his own teeth, dress himself, and be trusted to follow instructions. Now all that was gone.

I was more tired and more war weary than I had ever felt. For eleven years we had loved and cared for Jonny, rejoicing with every triumph and undeterred by temporary setbacks. This loss was different. It didn't feel like a temporary setback. It felt like defeat. I had never truly grieved for the loss of my son because I still had him. Now I was grieving as if he had been torn from my arms.

I knew in my head that I should be rejoicing. Jonathan could still say what was on his mind, and I now knew that he was capable of so much. During Jonny's recovery, the music minister had asked Jonny about his painting, and Jonny answered "Because God is with me!" Jonny hadn't been in isolation for eleven years. Jonny was never alone because Jesus was with him. I didn't need to pity Jonny; he wasn't alone now either. I thought of how he had prayed to Jesus during his recovery with such sincerity and ease. I knew that Jonny loves Jesus, and Jesus loves him even more than I do. I realized that I wasn't grieving for Jonny; I was grieving for me. Then the peace and joy that are found only in Christ Jesus drowned out even the mutterings of my own heart; I could suppress the desire to praise God no longer.

I will not be overcome by grief and mourning. I will not quit running the race when I can see the finish line. God is gracious and not just to Jonathan. He is gracious to all of us, and He showers us daily with undeserved blessings.

Kathleen R. Dale
April 18, 2015

The Dale Family

Left to right:
1st row Nicolai
2nd row Elizabeth, Mervin, Victoria, Devon, Jonathan, and Teddy
3rd row Alexandria, Cynthia, Kathleen, Yao, and Anthony

More about Jonny

Jonny's interview with WJCT can be viewed at www.youtube.com/watch?v=BK_P3KagSg0

Jonny has a website at www.artbyjonnydale.com

Jonny also has a facebook page. We invite you to like at www.facebook.com/storyofjon

Please feel free to contact us through the Art by Jonny Dale website listed above.

Special Thanks to Our Sponsors & Patrons

Thank you all for making it possible to publish Jonny's story. The financial backing was important, but the encouragement and love you provided was even more essential. We are blessed to count you as friends.

Sponsors

Donny Albritton
Jenny Alvarado
Melissa Carney
Pat Conway
Mark Culbreth
Bruce & Susan Curlett
Steven Danskine
Pamela Dix
John Gann
Georgina Georgescu
Jaqueline D. Harris
Megan Campbell Harris
Violeta Iglesias
Devon & Victoria Johnson
Mindy Johnson

Roger & Gloria Johnson
Kathryn
Emily Minich
John & Fran McCormick
Pam McElroy
Amber M. Summers
Christina SanInocencio
Marlane Soldner
Stephen & Marsha
Sutton
John Thomas
Allen & Karen
Vailliencourt
Oline Wright

Patrons

Marc & Shelly Florian
Jeff Meling
Jeff & Amy Register

www.ingramcontent.com/pod-product-compliance
Lightning Source LLC
LaVergne TN
LVHW072106070426
835509LV00002B/32